Banking

Money and Me

Banking

by
Joan Sobczak

Rourke Publications, Inc.
Vero Beach, FL 32964

Photo on page 2 by James L. Shaffer.

Produced by Salem Press, Inc.

Library of Congress Cataloging-in-Publication Data
Sobczak, Joan, 1959-
    Banking / by Joan Sobczak.
        p.   cm. — (Money and me)
    Includes bibliographical references and index.
    Summary: Explains how banks operate and the financial services they provide.
    ISBN 0-86625-608-3
    1. Banks and banking—Juvenile literature. 2. Finance, Personal— Juvenile literature. I. Title. II. Series.
HG1609.S65   1997
332.1—dc21   97-6367
                                                         CIP
                                                          AC

First Printing

PRINTED IN THE UNITED STATES OF AMERICA

Contents

What Is Banking?

Banking involves anything done with help from a bank. People open accounts with banks to save *money*. Other people go to banks to borrow money.

Penny Franklin, an elementary school student, often uses quarters from her allowance to buy bubblegum from a giant gumball machine at the grocery store. Her mother says that Penny would be rich if she had put all those quarters in the bank instead.

Penny used to put her allowance in her toy safe. She took money out of her safe when she wanted to buy something. The bank where her parents put money works the same way. People *deposit* money in the bank to save it, and they *withdraw* money when they want to buy something.

Why Use a Bank?

Why would you want to go to the bank instead of keeping your *cash* (such as paper bills and coins) at home? For one thing, money is safer if you deposit it in a bank. For another thing, the bank pays you extra money if you save there. The money that a bank pays you for saving is called *interest*. The more money you have in the bank, the more interest you earn.

When Penny heard about banks paying interest, she decided to empty her toy safe. She took her bills and coins to a bank to make her first bank deposit.

Savings Accounts

Banks have various types of *savings accounts*. Some types allow people to have a very small amount, or *balance*, in an account. Others require a bigger balance but pay a higher rate of interest.

Banks have different rules about allowing young people to open *savings accounts*, make *deposits*, and make *withdrawals* on their own. Penny's parents helped her to open her savings account, but the account has Penny's name on it.

Banks keep track of how much money each person deposits and withdraws. Banks do this by keeping separate records for each person. These records are called *accounts*.

Penny put all of her cash in her new savings account. A few weeks later, however, she wanted

Children are responsible for much of their own spending.
(James L. Shaffer)

to buy a pair of in-line skates. She knew she did not have enough money in the bank to afford skates. Penny asked her parents to lend her the money. She promised to pay them back, and they agreed to lend her the amount she needed.

If you have cash saved at home, you might want to start banking with a savings account. You will

Parents can help make decisions about bigger purchases. (PhotoDisc, Inc.)

get to see for yourself some of the ways banks work and help their customers.

Other Bank Services

Banks lend money to people, too. Borrowing money from a bank is called taking out a *loan*. Borrowers must pay back the loan and also pay the bank interest. A bank pays you interest for saving your money in an account at the bank. People must pay the bank interest if the bank gives them a loan. Banks make money by charging interest on loans.

Banks want to have enough paper bills and coins on hand to give to people when they make withdrawals from their bank accounts. Banks also need coins and paper bills to give to people who bring in checks, because a *check* tells the bank to give someone money from the check writer's account.

Penny got a $10 bill in a birthday card from her grandmother. She deposited the $10 into her savings account. She went back to the bank a few weeks later and withdrew $10 from her account to buy a backpack. What she received was a $10 bill that looked older and more wrinkled than the one her grandmother sent. She did not get back the same $10 bill her grandmother had sent because the bank uses people's deposits to give to other customers.

If you had $20 and wanted to save it in your savings account, you could go to the bank and deposit it. What if you had a diamond ring, an Olympic gold medal, or something else worth a lot of money? You also could put those things in a bank. They would go in a locked container and be kept inside the *vault* at the bank. The vault is a big safe, and the containers for valuable things are called *safe-deposit boxes*. Some people put important papers in safe-deposit boxes.

As you get older, you may want to do other kinds of banking besides using a savings account.

Maybe you will borrow money from the bank to buy a car or take out an even bigger loan to buy a house. Maybe you will need to write checks and will open your own checking account. You might have valuable things to put in a safe-deposit box. Banks help people in many ways besides these.

Different Ways of Banking

You will not always have to go inside the bank to do your banking. You might use an *automated*

Automated teller machines (ATMs) provide easy access to cash in your bank account. (James L. Shaffer)

A few banks allow customers to do some of their banking from home, through personal computers or telephones. (AP/ Wide World Photos)

teller machine (ATM). You would put a small plastic card that looks like a credit card into the machine and push buttons for your *personal identification number* (PIN). Your PIN is a secret number. You should not tell it to anyone, except maybe your parents. If someone tries to use your ATM card without the PIN, it will not work. That is how your PIN number protects your account.

You could use an ATM to withdraw cash from your account. The cash would come out of the machine. You also could deposit cash or checks written to you, see the balance of your account, pay back money on a loan, and more.

People also may do some banking by using a push-button telephone. Penny's uncle moves money from his savings account to his checking account by telephone. He also calls on the phone to use money from his bank account to pay bills. With a telephone and a PIN, people do some of their banking without even leaving the house.

Some customers use their home computers to connect to a bank's computer or a computer network. They may even open new bank accounts by computer. Not all banks have on-line banking for people with home computers. Penny wondered when her bank would get it.

Some customers like to talk to bank tellers to do their banking. Other customers prefer to use automated teller machines, telephones, or computers because these machines make banking convenient and speedy.

How Does Banking Work?

Penny Franklin made three deposits into her savings account. She wondered how much she had saved altogether and how much interest she had earned. When her first bank *statement* came in the mail, she found out. The bank statement is a report that shows the amount of each deposit and withdrawal, the amount of interest earned, and the total amount an account holder has in the bank.

Banks send statements of most accounts once a month. In between statements, people can find out exactly how much money they have in the bank. They can find out by talking to someone at the bank, or by using an automated teller machine, telephone, or home computer.

Penny has a statement savings account. Another type of savings account is a passbook account. The bank gives you a little book called a *passbook*. Every time you deposit or withdraw money from your account, you take the passbook with you. The bank records the amount of your deposit or withdrawal in the passbook. This information also goes into the bank's computer. The passbook shows the amount of interest earned and your total, or balance, in the account. Passbook savings accounts used to be common. Statement savings accounts are more common now.

Checks and Checking

Banks offer more than just savings accounts. Penny's uncle has a *checking account*. He deposits money into the checking account so that he may write checks. A check is a signed note that tells a bank to pay someone money from a checking account.

A BANK STATEMENT

Great First Bank

PENNY FRANKLIN
4321 N CALIFORNIA STREET
BURBANK CA 91504

SUMMARY

Statement Date:	**Oct. 10, 1997**
Beginning Balance:	232.16
Total Deposits:	+ 14.00
Total Withdrawals:	– 10.00
Service Fees:	– 0.00
Interest:	+ .58
Ending Balance:	236.74

STATEMENT SAVINGS ACCOUNT NUMBER: 98-76-5432

DATE	WITHDRAWALS	DEPOSITS	BALANCE
Sep. 12		10.00	242.16
Oct. 4		4.00	246.16
Oct. 8	10.00		236.16
Interest Paid 9/11/97 through 10/10/97:		.58	236.74
Interest Paid This Year:	$4.32		

3.03% Annual Percentage Yield   Interest Rate as of 9/11/97:
                                                          3.00%

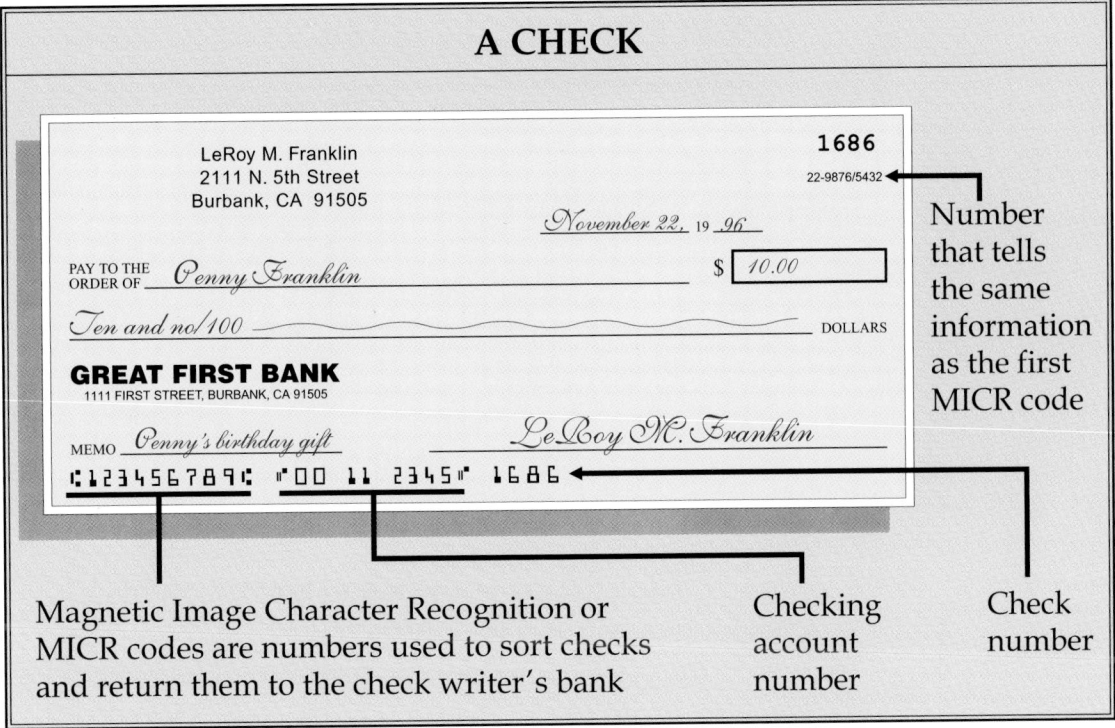

A CHECK

LeRoy M. Franklin
2111 N. 5th Street
Burbank, CA 91505

1686

22-9876/5432

November 22, 19 96

PAY TO THE ORDER OF _Penny Franklin_ $ 10.00

Ten and no/100 _____ DOLLARS

GREAT FIRST BANK
1111 FIRST STREET, BURBANK, CA 91505

MEMO _Penny's birthday gift_   _LeRoy M. Franklin_

⑆1234567 89⑆ ⑈00 11 2345⑈ 1686

Number that tells the same information as the first MICR code

Magnetic Image Character Recognition or MICR codes are numbers used to sort checks and return them to the check writer's bank

Checking account number

Check number

Penny's Uncle LeRoy sent her a check for her birthday. He wrote the date on a line at the top of the check. He wrote Penny's name on a line that says, "Pay to the Order of." That means her uncle wanted to pay Penny money. He wrote $10.00 in a small rectangle after the line with Penny's name. On another line, he wrote, "Ten and no/100." Those words show that her uncle really meant to pay Penny ten dollars and no cents. Her uncle had to sign his name at the bottom of the check. He also wrote a small note at the bottom of the check that says "Penny's birthday gift," to show why he gave her the check.

Checks come in books called checkbooks. A checkbook also has pages to keep track of how much money is in the checking account. This is very important so that people do not write checks unless they have enough money in the bank.

Sometimes, the pages to keep track of money in the checking account are with the checks. Other checkbooks have a separate little book called a

SAMPLE CHECK REGISTER

NUMBER	DATE	DESCRIPTION OF TRANSACTION	PAYMENT/DEBIT (−)	✓ T	FEE (IF ANY) (−)	DEPOSIT/CREDIT (+)	BALANCE
							$ 500 00
1686	11/22	Penny's birthday gift	$ 10 00		$	$	10 00
							490 00

check register. Penny's uncle had $500.00 in his checking account. He subtracted $10.00 when he wrote the check for Penny's birthday. His check register showed the original balance of $500.00, the $10.00 check, and the new balance of $490.00. It also showed the check number, which is different for each check and helps to identify it, the date that he wrote the check, and what the check was for.

When Penny received her uncle's check, she took it to her bank to cash it. She signed her name on the back of the check and gave it to her bank. Penny could get paper dollars for the check or deposit the $10 from her uncle's check into her savings account.

Her uncle's checking account is at another bank, and Penny's bank could not just take money out of his account for the check. Checks from accounts at different banks may get delivered to a Federal Reserve bank, a check clearinghouse, or a correspondent bank. These all are places where checks get sorted. The check that Penny's uncle wrote will soon get returned to his bank, and the amount of the check will be deducted from his account.

Numbers printed in special magnetic ink on the bottom of each check show where the check has to go and the amount of the check. Banking machines can read these magnetic numbers.

Penny's bank gave her $10 for her uncle's check. Her bank had the $10 added to its account, and the same amount got subtracted from the account of her uncle's bank. His bank subtracted the $10 from his individual checking account.

Other Types of Accounts

Savings accounts and some checking accounts earn interest. Some other kinds of bank accounts earn an even higher rate of interest.

Penny had $5 that she planned to put into her savings account. Her older brother wanted to go out on a date and asked Penny if he could borrow her $5. Penny said yes but made her brother write a note that said, "I owe you $5 by next week." Penny put this IOU (short for "I owe you") in her toy safe until her brother paid her back.

Banks offer something called a time *certificate of deposit*, or CD. A bank might not allow young people to buy CDs on their own.

A certificate of deposit (CD) may pay a higher rate of interest, but the depositor has limited access to the money. (Ben Klaffke)

CERTIFICATE OF DEPOSIT

SACRAMENTO COMMERCIAL BANK   701 0 8793   4

NOT NEGOTIABLE
NOT TRANSFERABLE

X MULTIPLE MATURITY   SINGLE MATURITY   Sacramento   CALIFORNIA   January 16, 19 97

THIS CERTIFIES THAT *** *** *** ***John Smith or Jane Smith*** *** *** *** *** *** ***   HAS/HAVE DEPOSITED

IN SACRAMENTO COMMERCIAL BANK One hundred thousand dollars and 00/100------ DOLLARS $ **100,000.00**

PAYABLE TO *** *** *** *** ***John Smith or Jane Smith*** *** *** *** *** *** *** *** ***

UPON SURRENDER OF THIS CERTIFICATE, PROPERLY ENDORSED.

This certificate is issued for a period of **365 days (Maturity 1-16-98)**. If multiple maturity it will automatically renew for a similar period of time, at the then current interest rate, unless presented for redemption with 10 days after the maturity date. The Bank reserves the right to redeem this certificate during any renewal period upon 14 days prior written notice. No interest will be paid on single maturity deposits after the maturity date.

Interest on this certificate shall be paid **at maturity** at the rate of **5.65** % per annum,

the X FIXED RATE ☐ VARIABLE RATE is adjusted **at maturity** based on the

bank's current interest rate upon maturity based on a **360**

day year X SIMPLE ☐ COMPOUNDED DAILY by, ☐ CREDIT TO ACCOUNT NO.

☐ PAYMENT TO OWNER OF RECORD X REINVEST UPON MATURITY (Multiple Maturity only)

A Substantial Penalty will be assessed for early withdrawal.   AUTHORIZED SIGNATURE

CD-003 (11/87)

If you buy a time CD, you get a piece of paper showing that you bought it. This paper works like Penny's IOU from her brother. It says that the bank will pay you the amount you deposited for the CD, plus interest. The bank agrees to pay you back on a certain day.

If you have a one-year CD, you tell your bank what you want to do with it at the end of the year. You have three main choices:

- Tell the bank that you want to renew it. This means that you want the CD for another year. You may not get the same rate of interest as you had before.

- Deposit the amount of the CD and the interest it earned into a different bank account.

- Tell the bank that you want to withdraw the amount of the CD and the interest.

Your bank may offer *money market accounts*. The interest rate on these accounts might change from week to week. Customers hope that the interest rates will be high. Banks allow deposits and withdrawals from these accounts. People may write a limited number of checks using money from their money market accounts, too.

Some people buy United States *savings bonds* at banks. A savings bond that costs $25 has a "face value" of $50 printed on it. It becomes worth that amount later by earning interest from the United States government. If you hold onto a $50 savings bond long enough, you can even get more than $50 for it because of the interest. Savings bonds also come with other face values.

Banks can help people set up savings accounts for special reasons. An *individual retirement account* (IRA) helps grown-ups save for the time when they retire from their jobs. Christmas Club accounts help people save to buy holiday gifts. People at your bank can tell you about different types of accounts and how they work.

Loans

A bank needs people to save money because the bank uses some of this money to give loans to other customers. People who take out loans pay back the amount of the loan, and they pay the bank interest. Banks lend money to individuals, businesses, and even governments.

Banks take care to lend to people who will not *default* on loans. Defaulting means not paying back a loan. Before making a loan, the bank will ask if the customer has a steady job and other questions to decide if the person should get a loan.

There might be something worth money that the bank could take over if the customer defaulted. Maybe the person has a house or a car or is buying one with the loan. Whatever the customer says the bank could take over is called *collateral*. Sometimes another person agrees to pay if the person who gets the loan defaults. This person is called a co-signer. The signed agreement from a co-signer is another kind of collateral.

Mortgages

When Penny's parents bought their home, they could not afford to pay for it all at once. They had saved $20,000, but the house cost $110,000. They

---

TYPES OF CONSUMER LOANS

- Mortgage
    Fixed-rate
    Adjustable-rate
- Automobile
- Personal (unsecured)
- Home Equity
- Credit Card or Charge Card

had to take out a loan for the other $90,000. Banks call a loan to buy a house a *mortgage loan*. The house is the collateral on a mortgage loan.

A mortgage loan agreement states several things about the loan. It tells the amount of the loan, the interest rate, and the number of years the borrower will take to pay back the loan.

Penny's parents pay 10% interest to the bank on their mortgage loan. They agreed to make payments each month for 30 years. Each monthly payment is about $790. They will pay

Because homes are so expensive, many buyers must take out mortgage loans. (Jim Whitmer)

EXAMPLES OF DIFFERENT MORTGAGES

Interest Rate	Amount of Loan	Number of Years	Monthly Payment	Total Payments	Total Amount of Interest
8%	$90,000	30	$660	$237,600	$147,600
8%	$90,000	15	$860	$154,800	$64,800
10%	$90,000	30	$790	$284,400	$194,400
10%	$90,000	15	$967	$174,100	$84,100

Note: Dollar amounts in the table are rounded.

the bank a total of more than $284,000 in those 30 years. Of that total, more than $194,000 is interest — more than two-thirds!

Most mortgages are made for either 30 years or 15 years, but some banks offer other time periods. They might also allow the interest rate on the mortgage to change while the loan is being paid back. Penny's parents have a *fixed-rate* mortgage. The interest rate will always be 10%, guaranteed. An *adjustable-rate* mortgage has an interest rate that can change, within some limits. While someone is paying back a mortgage, interest rates on all sorts of loans might rise. By taking out an adjustable-rate mortgage, the borrower agrees to pay a higher rate of interest on the mortgage if other interest rates go up. If other interest rates go down, the interest rate on the mortgage goes down too.

People get to live in their houses while they pay back their mortgage loans. Most people could never afford to buy homes if they had to pay for them all at once instead of getting a mortgage loan to pay back a little at a time.

Other Types of Loans

New cars cost many thousands of dollars. People often use loans to buy cars. *Automobile* or *car*

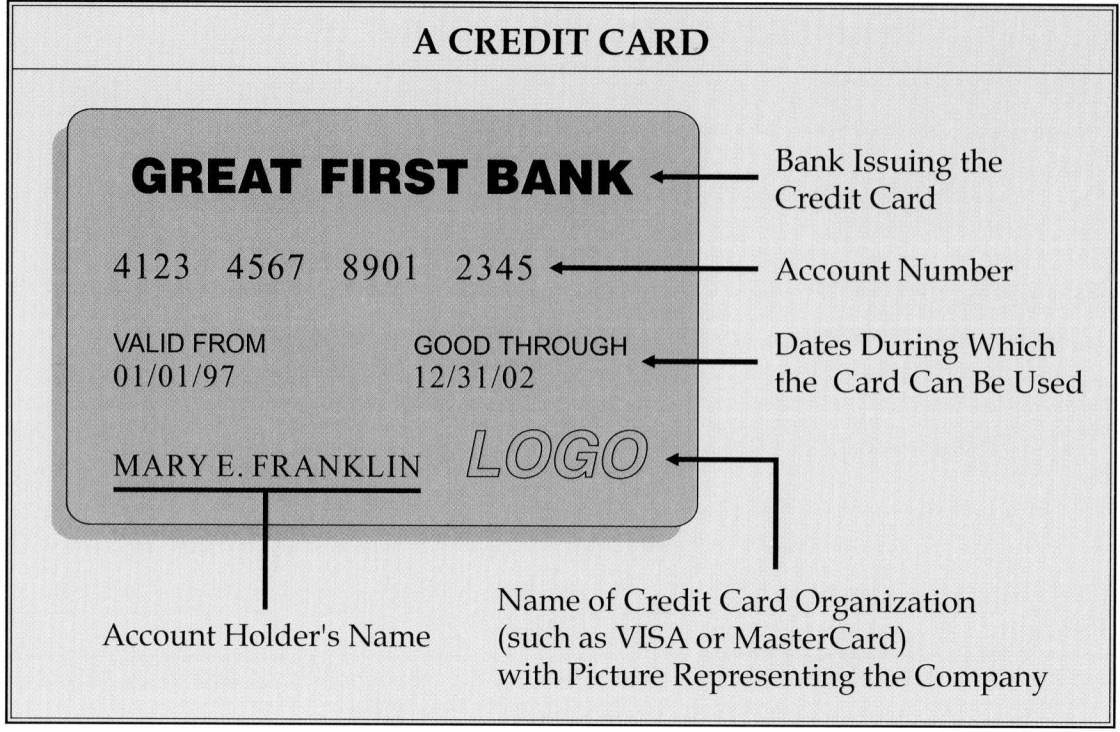

A CREDIT CARD

GREAT FIRST BANK ← Bank Issuing the Credit Card

4123   4567   8901   2345 ← Account Number

VALID FROM   GOOD THROUGH   Dates During Which
01/01/97   12/31/02   the Card Can Be Used

MARY E. FRANKLIN   *LOGO*

Account Holder's Name

Name of Credit Card Organization
(such as VISA or MasterCard)
with Picture Representing the Company

loans help people make these expensive purchases. Banks make money on the interest people pay on these loans. Sometimes, automobile companies offer loans to people who buy their cars.

Penny's family needed a new refrigerator and stove. Her parents got a *personal loan* from the bank. People use personal loans to make many kinds of purchases. Sometimes these are called *unsecured loans* because they do not require *collateral*. When deciding whether to make a personal loan, the bank would look at your ability to repay the loan. It would ask how much money you make and what you owe to other people already.

Another kind of loan is a *home equity loan*. People can borrow up to a certain amount of money for whatever they want to buy, but they must own a home to get the loan. The home is *collateral*.

Using Credit

Some banks offer *credit cards* as another type of loan. A credit card or charge card is a small rectangle made out of plastic that has an account number on it. Using a credit card is like taking out a loan. The bank sets a limit on how much a person can owe on a credit card. If a person reaches his or her *credit limit*, the bank will not allow that person to use the card anymore until some of the account balance is paid back.

Penny's mother used her credit card to pay for new school clothes for Penny. Her mother gave the credit card to the store clerk. The clerk put the card into a machine to print out a sales slip for Penny's mother to sign. By signing her name, Penny's mother promised to pay for the clothes later.

Penny's mother will get a bill in the mail. If she does not pay the bill soon, she will have to pay her bank interest, plus paying for Penny's school clothes. She plans to pay the bill on time to avoid paying interest. She could have paid cash for the clothes, but using the credit card was more convenient.

Who Does What?

For Career Day at school, Penny decided to report on careers in banking. She found out about lots of different jobs and wondered which ones she might like to have if she worked at a bank one day.

When Penny deposits money at the bank, she talks to a *teller*. The teller counts Penny's money, types the amount of the deposit into a computer, and gives Penny a receipt to show how much she deposited.

Bank tellers help many people do their everyday, routine banking. They also try to sell bank services

Tellers handle most everyday banking needs other than automated banking. (James L. Shaffer)

to customers. For example, if a customer has a savings account, the teller might encourage the person to open a checking account, too.

Each bank teller has a drawer with cash in it at the bank. The teller must carefully count the cash given to customers. Otherwise, the teller will have too little or too much money in the drawer at the end of the day. If the teller has exactly the right amount, the drawer "balances." Drawers should balance every day.

Penny likes typing on computers. She has a friendly personality, too. She thought that she might enjoy being a bank teller.

Who Makes the Loans?

Bank *loan officers* help people who want to borrow money from a bank. They talk to people about the kinds of loans they need. Is the loan for a house? A car? A new stove and refrigerator? Is it for college?

Here are some of the other questions a loan officer uses to decide if a person should get a loan:

- How much do you want to borrow?
- How long will you need to pay back the loan and interest?
- Where do you work?
- How long have you worked there?
- How much do you earn each year?
- Do you have any other loans right now?
- Is there something the bank could take over if you do not pay back your loan? (The loan officer would call this collateral.)

Businesses borrow money from banks, too. The bank employees who approve business loans must understand business reports. That way, they can decide if a business will be able to repay a loan that it takes out.

Penny thought it would be fun to figure out who should get loans, but at some banks,

☒ SACRAMENTO COMMERCIAL BANK ☒

LOAN APPLICATION/PERSONAL FINANCIAL STATEMENT

INSTRUCTIONS: You may apply for a loan in your name alone, regardless of your marital status. If you are married, but your spouse is not applying for a loan with you, please carefully read the following instructions before you complete this application.

a. You do not have to give information on your spouse if you base your application only on your SEPARATE property or income from it.
b. To include community property (such as your salary or that of your spouse), you must complete information on your spouse.

THIS IS AN APPLICATION FOR ☐ JOINT / ☐ SEPARATE CREDIT AMOUNT REQUESTED $ _____ OFFICE _____

PURPOSE OF LOAN
If it is for the purchase or improvement of your residence, is it your primary residence?

APPLICANT INFORMATION

NAME ____ ADDRESS ____ ZIP ____

TELEPHONE ____ AGE ____ ☐ MARRIED ☐ UNMARRIED ☐ SEPARATED SOCIAL SECURITY NUMBER ____ OCCUPATION ____

EMPLOYER ____ BUSINESS ADDRESS ____ ZIP ____ TELEPHONE ____

NET SALARY OR COMM ____ PER ____ NUMBER OF YEARS THERE ____

CO-APPLICANT/SPOUSE INFORMATION

CO-APPLICANT'S NAME ____ SOCIAL SECURITY NUMBER ____ OCCUPATION ____

EMPLOYER ____ BUSINESS ADDRESS ____ ZIP ____ TELEPHONE ____

NET SALARY OR COMM ____ PER ____ NUMBER OF YEARS THERE ____

FINANCIAL CONDITION AS OF ____, 19 ____

ASSETS	AMOUNT	LIABILITIES	AMOUNT
CASH (Schedule 1)		NOTES PAYABLE - BANKS (Schedule 5)	
STOCKS & BONDS (Schedule 2)		MARGIN ACCOUNT	
REAL ESTATE (Schedule 3)		CHATTEL MORTGAGES (Auto, etc.)	
RECEIVABLES (Schedule 4)		REAL ESTATE LOANS (Schedule 3)	
AUTO: Make Yr.		TAXES OWING	
Make Yr.		OTHER LIABILITIES (Schedule 5)	
OTHER ASSETS		TOTAL LIABILITIES	
		NET WORTH	
TOTAL	$	TOTAL	$

Please attach a separate sheet if you need more space to complete a schedule. For all schedules, please indicate ownership as follows:
C = Community Property   JT = Joint Tenancy   S = Separate Property   TC = Tenants in Common

SCHEDULE 1: CASH

CHKG	SVGS	BANK OR S&L	ADDRESS	ACCOUNT NO.	BALANCE	ACCT. IN NAME OF	OWNERSHIP CODE

SCHEDULE 2: LISTED AND UNLISTED STOCKS AND BONDS (ARE ANY OF THE BELOW SECURITIES PLEDGED, OR ARE YOU AWARE OF ANY RESTRICTIONS ON THEIR SALE?) ☐ YES ☐ NO If yes, give details

NAME/SYMBOL	WHERE LISTED	NUMBER OF SHARES OR PAR VALUE	OWNERSHIP CODE	% OWNED	ISSUED IN NAME(S) OF	MARKET VALUE

SCHEDULE 3: REAL ESTATE OWNED Indicate: I - Improved   U - Unimproved

STREET ADDRESS AND TYPE OF IMPROVEMENT	TITLE IN NAME(S) OF	OWNER-SHIP CODE	% OWNED	YEAR ACQU.	COST	PRESENT VALUE	TRUST DEED MORTGAGES OR OTHER LIENS			HELD BY
							UNPAID BALANCE	RATE %	MONTHLY PAYMENT	

SCHEDULE 4: ACCOUNTS, NOTES AND TRUST DEEDS RECEIVABLE

DUE FROM	HOW PAID	BALANCE DUE	FINAL MATURITY	OWNERSHIP CODE	COLLATERAL

computers make that decision. The loan officer helps a customer fill out the form to ask for a loan and explains what other papers the bank needs. Then, a computer uses this information to figure out if the person should get the loan. At other banks, the loan officer decides about small loans, but a group of people at the bank decides who should get bigger loans. With a group, more people have to agree about these important decisions.

Trust Accounts and Officers

Bank *trust officers* help people with trust accounts. Trust accounts are set up so that someone called a trustee has power to handle the money in the account. A bank can be a trustee. The person who actually gets money from the account is called the *beneficiary*.

Penny's grandparents set up a trust account to give Penny money for college. Her grandparents want the trust officer at their bank to invest the money wisely. *Investing* means putting money where it can earn more money, for example by earning interest.

Penny's grandparents considered several options for Penny's trust account. They wanted the money to earn a high rate of interest, but they also wanted it to be safe. The trust officer suggested putting the money into a certificate of deposit (CD). The CD would be insured and earn a higher rate of interest than a savings account.

WALTER WRISTON

A bank in New York with the nickname Citibank was the first to sell an important banking invention called the negotiable certificate of deposit. These "jumbo" certificates of deposit sell for $100,000 or more, and often for $1,000,000 each.

One of the inventors, Walter B. Wriston, believed that these CDs would help the bank grow. He was right.

First National City Bank officially changed its name to Citibank in 1976. By then, Wriston had worked his way up to being chairman of the bank and its parent company.

Wriston started as a junior inspector at the bank. Later, he met with United States presidents about issues related to money. He also became chairman of the U.S. president's Economic Policy Advisory Board. He retired in 1984 as a famous banker.

The trust officer also may work with *wills*. A will tells what to do with someone's money and belongings after the person dies.

Bank employees have certain jobs to do. An *operations manager* makes sure that these jobs get done in an organized way. The operations manager also thinks about how the bank should use computers and other machines. At large banks, each department may have its own operations manager.

Your bank may have an *investment sales representative*. This person sells *securities* to people. Securities are bonds and other investments that a person might buy. The investment sales representative explains different types of securities to people. Penny thought that she might like to learn about securities and help people buy them.

Many other people work at banks. Some have clerical jobs. This means that they type, keep records, and use office machines. They may have many different job titles, such as clerk, bookkeeper, machine operator, administrative assistant, or secretary. Some people start their banking careers in clerical jobs and later get promoted.

Penny thought that she might like to be the head person at a bank. Some banks have a chairperson and a president. Other banks have one person with both jobs. They solve problems and think of ways the bank could run better. They meet with people to try to get new customers for the bank. For example, the head of Penny's bank tries to meet people from different companies. The companies and their employees may open accounts or get loans from the bank.

Banks have other people who are bosses in parts of the bank. They may be called vice presidents or department heads.

The bank where Penny has her account is called a *branch bank*. That means the bank has more than

one location or branch. Banks have branches so that people will not need to go far to get to the bank. The branch manager makes sure that employees do their jobs so that the branch runs the way it should.

Some people who work at banks do not help people with banking but still have important jobs. For example, banks have security officers and security guards. They protect the bank from robbers and from people who might try to trick the bank about the amount of deposits or withdrawals.

Most banks have several branches, so that customers have a convenient location at which to do their banking. **(Ben Klaffke)**

Watching Over the Bank

Bank examiners may work for the federal (U.S.) or state government. Many work for the Federal Reserve Banks. They have the important job of making sure that banks obey banking laws and use money safely. For example, bank examiners check to see if banks make too many loans to customers who are likely to default. Penny thought that she would enjoy traveling to different banks instead of working in one place.

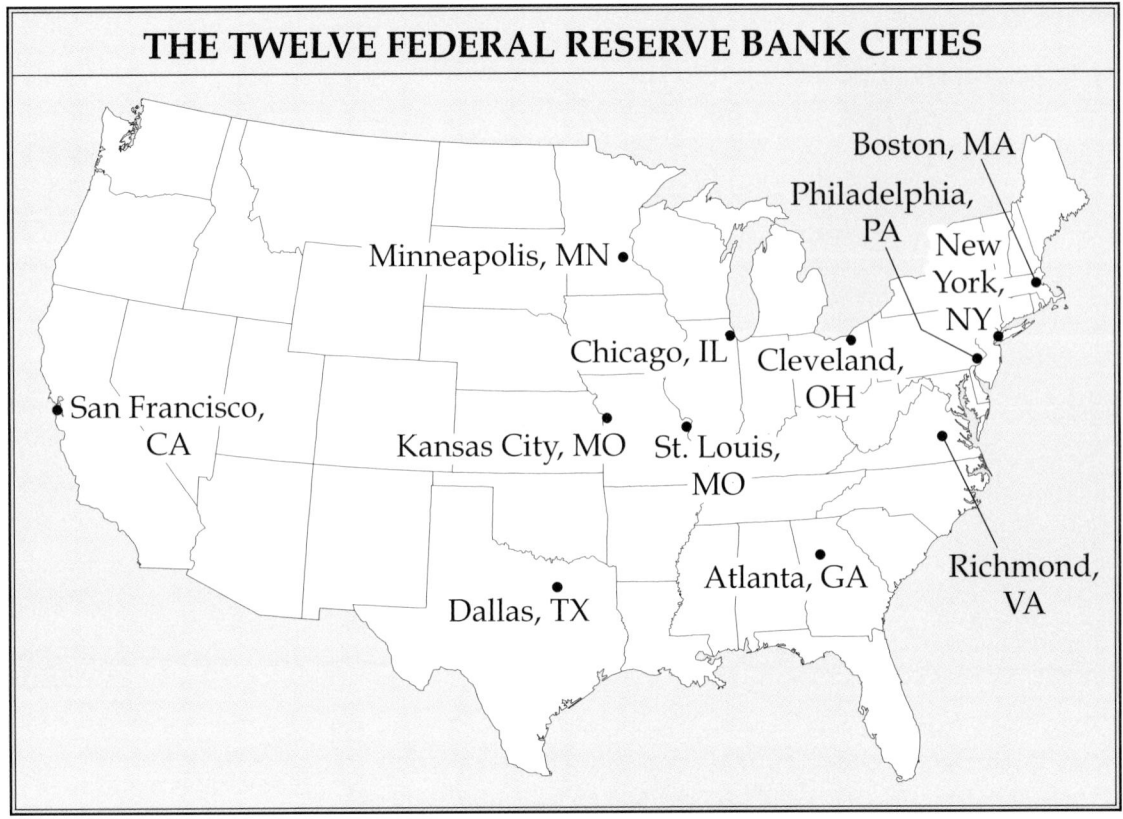

THE TWELVE FEDERAL RESERVE BANK CITIES

Boston, MA
Philadelphia, PA
New York, NY
Minneapolis, MN
Chicago, IL
Cleveland, OH
San Francisco, CA
Kansas City, MO
St. Louis, MO
Richmond, VA
Atlanta, GA
Dallas, TX

Penny learned that instead of one main bank, the United States has the *Federal Reserve System*. The Federal Reserve System has twelve main banks in different cities around the country. There are also twenty-five branch banks and thousands of member banks.

The Federal Reserve banks do not print new paper money. The United States Treasury does this. Worn-out paper money is destroyed and replaced with new money. Damaged coins are melted down to make new ones.

Many banks in the United States do not belong to the Federal Reserve System. Some banks, called national banks, must belong. Other banks make a choice to become members of the Federal Reserve System. Member banks must pay a fee, but they get some privileges. Penny decided to ask someone at her bank if it belongs to the Federal Reserve System.

ALAN GREENSPAN

In 1987, President Ronald Reagan picked Alan Greenspan to be the new chairman of the Federal Reserve System's Board of Governors. Presidents Bush and Clinton renominated him. You may find it surprising that Greenspan did not work at a bank before getting this job.

Greenspan was born in New York City in 1926. He has a doctorate degree in economics from New York University.

Before he began working for the Federal Reserve System, Greenspan was in business as an economist. He had also been chairman of the U.S. president's Council of Economic Advisers. Among other things, economists like Greenspan try to figure out what people will do with their money in the future. Will they spend or save their extra money? What kinds of investments will they make? Will they want to take out loans?

The Federal Reserve System controls the amount of money available in the United States. One way it does this is by buying or selling government securities. Greenspan's job as chairman of the Federal Reserve's Board of Governors has to do with money, the economy, and banking.

Alan Greenspan often speaks to congresspeople about laws affecting banking. (AP/Wide World Photos)

CHAPTER 4

What Are the Rules?

People use banks to keep their money in a safe place. They earn interest on their money, too. Banks have different rules about how much money you need to open accounts and how much interest you get.

Banks call the amount of money you need to open an account the *minimum balance* . For example, you may need at least $100 to open a savings account at your bank. Some banks have special rules about minimum opening balances for children's accounts. A minimum balance also may mean the lowest account balance a person can have without having to pay a fee or losing interest.

Each bank decides how much interest to pay customers on passbook or statement savings accounts. Things get even more complicated because banks do not figure out interest the same way. The bank must tell you the interest rate you will actually earn per year. Some banks count a year as 365 days. Other banks use 360 days or 366 days.

Banks keep some of the money people deposit on reserve. They also have special rules in case too many people want to make withdrawals at the same time. Customers may have to tell a bank in

advance that they plan to withdraw money. These
rules exist only for emergencies and for very large
withdrawals. Penny has always gotten her money
right away each time she made a withdrawal.

    Penny deposited a check that her aunt sent for
her birthday. She realized that her bank would not
get the money right away from her aunt's check.
When you deposit money from a check into your
savings account, you might have to wait several
days before you can withdraw it again. You should
ask the bank teller if you want to know how soon
you will be able to withdraw money deposited
from a check.

Banks may require advance notice if customers want to withdraw large amounts of money. (Ben Klaffke)

Choosing a Checking Account

    Some checking accounts earn interest, and
some do not. Penny wondered why a person
would choose a checking account that does not
pay interest. She found out by talking to two of
her cousins.

Cousin Mitch's checking account does not have a minimum balance. His bank, however, charges $5 every month for Mitch to have the account. He also does not earn any interest.

Cousin Deirdre earns interest on the money in her checking account. There is a minimum balance of $500 to avoid fees. If she goes below that minimum balance, Deirdre must pay the bank $5 per month plus 25 cents for every check she writes.

Last month, Cousin Mitch wrote five checks. He only had to pay the bank $5 for his checking account that month. Cousin Deirdre wrote five checks, too. She did not have the $500 minimum balance in her account. She had to pay the bank $5, and she had to pay 25 cents for each check she wrote. Altogether, Deirdre had to pay the bank $6.25 for having her checking account. She only earned 41 cents in interest. That month, she wished that she had a no-interest checking account like Cousin Mitch's. Then, she would have had to pay the bank only $5. Instead, she paid $6.25 and earned 41 cents in interest. The difference between the $6.25 she paid and the 41 cents she earned in interest was $5.84. That was how much it really cost her to have her checking account that month.

Which Type of Account?

Banks may change the interest rates on savings, checking, and money market accounts. Once you buy a time certificate of deposit, however, you know that you will get a guaranteed rate of interest for the entire time you have it.

If you withdraw money from a time CD early, the bank can charge a penalty, such as three months of interest. Each bank decides how much the penalty will be. People should not buy these CDs if they want to make deposits and withdrawals whenever they want. Other types of CDs have different rules.

Banks offer special savings accounts for people to save money for retirement. Penny's grandfather set up an individual retirement account (IRA) a long time ago at his bank. He kept saving money in this special bank account. When he stopped working, he began to use this money to pay his

Customer service representatives help people choose which accounts will be best for them. (Ben Klaffke)

A car can be the collateral for the loan used to buy it.
(James L. Shaffer)

bills and buy things. Individual retirement accounts have large penalties for withdrawing money before retirement.

Rules About Loans

Banks have rules about loans, too. When someone gets a loan from a bank, the person must promise to pay it back on time and pay the bank interest.

Penny wanted to know what would happen if someone broke the promise to pay back a loan. A loan officer explained to her that banks ask for *collateral* in case that happens. Collateral is something the bank can take over, or it is someone else's signed promise to pay if the person who got the loan defaults.

Foreclosure happens when a bank takes over a house because the buyer does not pay back a mortgage loan. Penny wondered if someone at the bank gets to live in the house when the bank takes it over. The answer is no. Instead, the house is sold, and the bank gets money from the sale.

A person who wants a loan for a car may use the car as collateral. The bank can *repossess* the car if the person does not repay the loan. That means the car is taken away from the person and sold. The bank gets money from selling the car.

People use personal loans from banks to buy many different things. If a borrower does not pay back a personal loan, the bank sometimes puts a *lien* on the person's house. This means that the person cannot sell the house until the personal loan is paid back.

Someone who buy things with a credit card must pay a bill that comes in the mail later. Liens are also used when people do not pay credit card bills.

Penny opened her savings account at the bank her parents use. She can ride along when they go to the bank. When you choose a bank on your own, it will pay to shop around to find the best interest rates and other rules for the kind of account or loan you need.

CHAPTER 5

Safety Features in Banking

Penny thought that her money would be safer in the bank than at home. She panicked when she heard about a bank robbery on the radio. What would happen if a robber came and robbed her bank? Would her savings be stolen?

Banks keep on hand only a small part of the money that people deposit. A bank robber could never steal all the money deposited at the bank, because the bank does not have it there.

Keeping Your Money Safe

Bank security guards protect people and their deposits from the kinds of bank robbers who wear masks and carry guns. Banks also worry about a more sneaky kind of robber. These robbers steal by fraud. Fraud means lying to the bank. A bank customer might try to convince the bank that the receipt from an ATM has the wrong amount on it. Banks have security officers and cameras on the lookout for fraud.

Even if Penny's bank closed, people would not lose the money they deposited. The *Federal Deposit Insurance Corporation*, also called the FDIC,

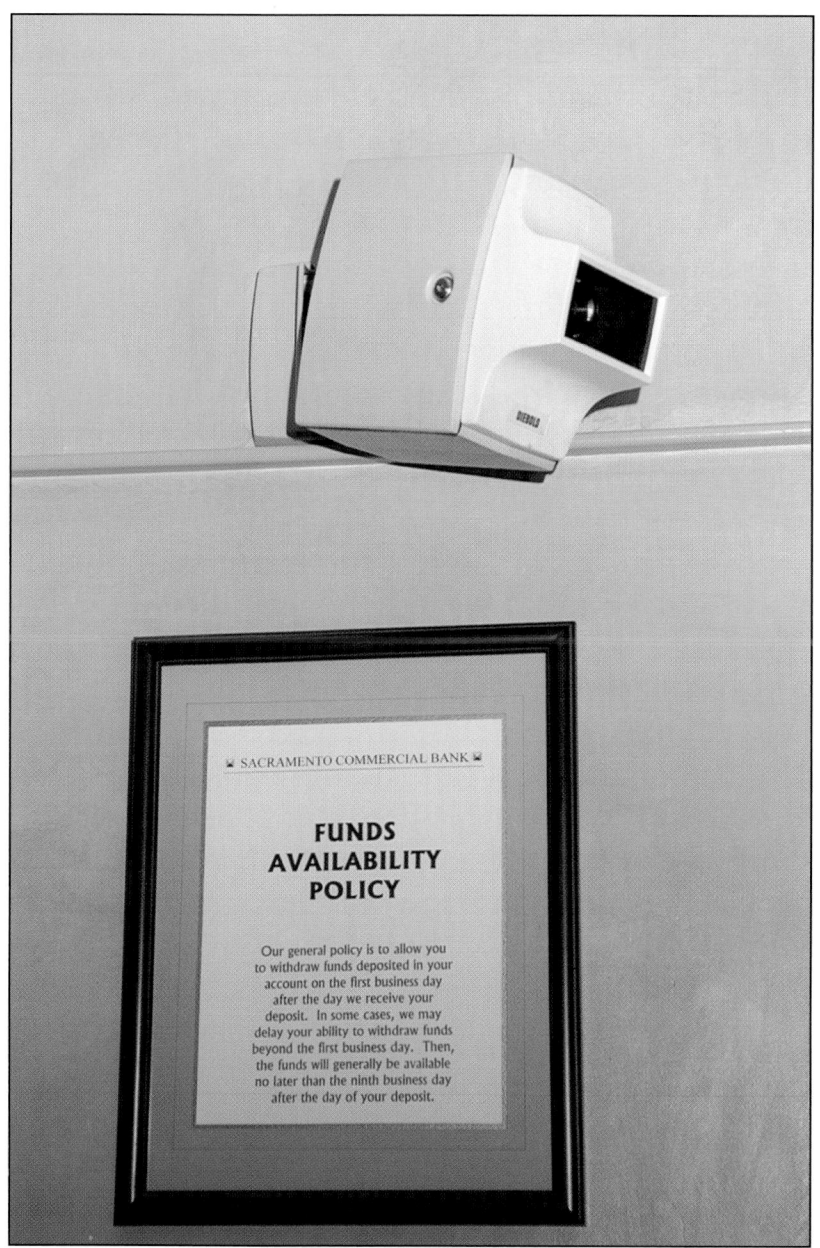

*Banks use cameras
and other electronic
devices such as
alarms to protect
their customers.
(Ben Klaffke)*

insures up to $100,000 deposited by one person in
the bank.

If the bank closes, the FDIC may find a different
bank for the deposits. Customers will still have
accounts, but at a new bank. Otherwise, the FDIC
will pay depositors their money. Even if the FDIC
fund did not have enough money to pay all the
depositors, the United States government promises
to pay.

Types of Banks

Penny went with a friend of hers named Amanda to make a deposit in Amanda's account. Penny thought they would be going to a bank. Instead, they went to a *savings and loan*.

When savings and loans began, the idea was to encourage people to save money. They would take turns borrowing money to build homes. Today, savings and loans offer different types of accounts. They also give loans to people who need money for college or other reasons besides buying homes. They even make loans to businesses.

Some people call savings and loans "thrifts" because a person who saves money is thrifty. Savings banks are also called thrifts.

Savings banks began back in the 1800's to help people save even if they could deposit only small amounts. Most U.S. savings banks are in the Northeast. These banks offer savings accounts and mortgage loans. People who work there can tell you what other services a particular savings bank offers.

Commercial banks used to have only businesses as customers. Now, anyone can use commercial banks. Some people call commercial banks full-service

Both businesses and ordinary people can take advantage of the wide range of services offered by commercial banks. (Ben Klaffke)

banks because of all the things they do. These services range from having safe-deposit boxes to helping businesses that buy or sell in other countries.

One day, Penny's mother agreed to pick up a friend of hers from work. Penny waited with her mother in the car. When the friend came out, she asked, "Would you mind if I go across the street to the *credit union*? I need to deposit my paycheck."

Penny had never heard of a credit union. Her mother explained that credit unions help people in many of the same ways as banks, but only certain people can use credit unions. For example, people who work at the same company might have a credit union. Workers from another company could not use it. Sometimes, members of the same church or the same community have their own credit unions.

The fact that people could do their banking at different kinds of banks and at places besides banks surprised Penny. Credit unions, savings and loans, and banks are all places to save money and get loans. They have different names for the insurance that covers deposits, but they usually insure each depositor for up to $100,000.

Choosing Where to Bank

How do people decide where to do their banking? They may look for a place close to home or work. They find out about interest rates and minimum balances. They should always ask about the FDIC or other insurance on deposits.

Sometimes, people want services such as automatic deposit of their paychecks. Customers may want the bank to pay their monthly bills automatically by taking money out of their bank accounts. Some people want to buy securities. Banks and other savings places will answer questions about what services they offer.

The more she learned, the more Penny liked the idea of banking instead of keeping cash at home in

A bank vault may contain safe-deposit boxes as well as cash and bank records. (Ben Klaffke)

her toy safe. She definitely liked to earn interest. Penny was also glad that somebody else could use her money by getting a loan from the bank.

By giving people loans, Penny realized that banks create money without the government printing any more paper bills or coins. Money means cash or amounts in accounts that are available to spend. Penny's parents borrowed $1,000 to buy their new stove and refrigerator. Imagine that Mary Greene has an account at the bank, and the bank used part of Mary's savings to give the loan to Penny's parents. Mary could still withdraw $1,000 from her account and spend it. Penny's parents also had $1,000 to spend. The bank created an extra $1,000 of money.

Penny has not decided if she wants to work at a bank someday. She definitely has decided that she wants to keep her money where it stays safe, earns interest, and helps people who need loans. She plans to keep on banking.

Glossary

account: A record for each person with money in the bank.

automated teller machine (ATM): A machine used to make deposits or withdrawals from an account, move money between accounts, and do some other banking.

balance: The amount of money in an account.

bank statement: *See* "statement."

banking: Anything a person does with help from a bank. People also use the word "banking" when they talk about savings and loans or credit unions, because those businesses do many of the same things as banks.

cash: Usually means paper bills and coins. In the United States, the bills are in dollar amounts. Most coins are worth a fraction of a dollar.

certificate of deposit (CD): A receipt for a deposit that will receive a certain rate of interest. Someone who has a time certificate of deposit agrees to deposit money for a certain length of time. There are other kinds of CDs besides time certificates of deposit.

check: A note telling a bank to pay someone money from the checking account of the person who wrote the check.

check register: Used to keep track of how much money someone has in a checking account. It has spaces to write information about each check and the checking account balance.

checkbook: A pad of checks and a check register together.

checking account: A record, kept by the bank, of how much money a person has on deposit to use for writing checks.

collateral: Something that a bank can take over if a customer does not pay back a loan. Sometimes, another person agrees to pay back the loan. This signed agreement is also collateral.

default: Failure to pay back a loan and interest.

deposit: Money put into an account, or the act of putting money into an account.

Federal Deposit Insurance Corporation (FDIC): A government agency that insures deposits in banks and savings and loans. If a bank or savings and loan closes, depositors can still get their money because the FDIC insures it.

Federal Reserve System: A group of twelve main banks, twenty-five branch banks, and thousands of member banks.

foreclosure: The way a bank takes over a house because a person fails to pay back a mortgage loan.

interest: Money paid by banks to depositors, or money paid to banks by people who get loans.

lien: Stops someone from selling property, such as a house, until that person pays back a loan.

loan: Borrowed money.

minimum balance: Amount of money needed to open an account or to avoid fees or penalties. The minimum balance to avoid fees or penalties may be different from the minimum balance to open the account.

money: Cash or amounts in accounts that are available to spend.

money market account: Account earning interest at rates that may change very often.

mortgage loan: Money borrowed to buy a home.

passbook: Small book showing deposits, withdrawals, interest, and the balance in a savings account. Some banks do not have passbook accounts anymore.

repossess: To take something that is collateral for a loan. (Bankers use the word *foreclosure* for repossessing a house.)

safe-deposit box: A locked container kept in the vault at a bank. People put important papers, jewelry, or other things in safe-deposit boxes.

savings account: A record of deposits, withdrawals, interest, and the current account balance. There are statement savings accounts and passbook savings accounts.

securities: Investments such as bonds (which pay interest) or stocks (which may pay dividends). A piece of paper (or maybe a computer entry) shows what type of security a person bought.

statement: A report showing deposits, withdrawals, interest, and the balance of an account.

vault: A big safe.

withdrawal: Money taken out of an account, or *withdrawn* from it.

Sources

Adler, David A. *Banks: Where the Money Is*. New York: Franklin Watts, 1985. The author tells the history of banking and some of the basics of banking today. Topics include how banks "create" money and why banks are safe places to save money.

Briers, Audrey. *Money*. New York: Bookwright Press, 1987. Talks about barter (trading things for each other), money, and banking. Topics include checking accounts, credit cards, and getting money to spend in other countries.

Cantwell, Lois. *Money and Banking*. New York: Franklin Watts, 1984. The first part explains the history of money, and the second part tells about banking. There is an interesting chapter on coin collecting. For older readers (7th or 8th grade).

Dolan, Edward F., Jr. *Money Talk*. New York: Julian Messner, 1986. This is an easy-to-understand dictionary of words that have to do with money and banking.

Maestro, Betsy. *The Story of Money*. New York: Clarion Books, 1993. Traces the development of money and banking back to early civilization. It takes the reader to colonial times in America and up to modern times. For 4th to 6th grade readers.

Wallace, David. *Money Basics*. Englewood Cliffs, N.J.: Prentice-Hall, 1984. Discusses how banks work, what government does in banking, loans, checks, and credit cards. Readers will also learn about other topics related to money. For older readers (6th to 8th grade).

Resource

Young Americans Bank, 311 Steele Street, Denver, CO 80206, telephone: (303) 321-2265. This bank is for people under eighteen years of age. It offers savings accounts, checking accounts, credit cards, and even loans. Children have accounts with their parents but do the banking. People can use the bank by mail if they do not live nearby.

Index